GALAXY OF SUPERSTARS

98°	Hanson
Aerosmith	Jennifer Love Hewitt
Ben Affleck	Faith Hill
Jennifer Aniston	Lauryn Hill
Backstreet Boys	Heath Ledger
Drew Barrymore	Jennifer Lopez
Beck	Ricky Martin
Brandy	Ewan McGregor
Garth Brooks	Mike Myers
Mariah Carey	'N Sync
Matt Damon	Gwyneth Paltrow
Dave Matthews Band	LeAnn Rimes
Destiny's Child	Adam Sandler
Cameron Diaz	Will Smith
Leonardo DiCaprio	Britney Spears
Céline Dion	Spice Girls
Dixie Chicks	Ben Stiller
Sarah Michelle Gellar	Jonathan Taylor Thomas
Tom Hanks	Venus Williams

CHELSEA HOUSE PUBLISHERS

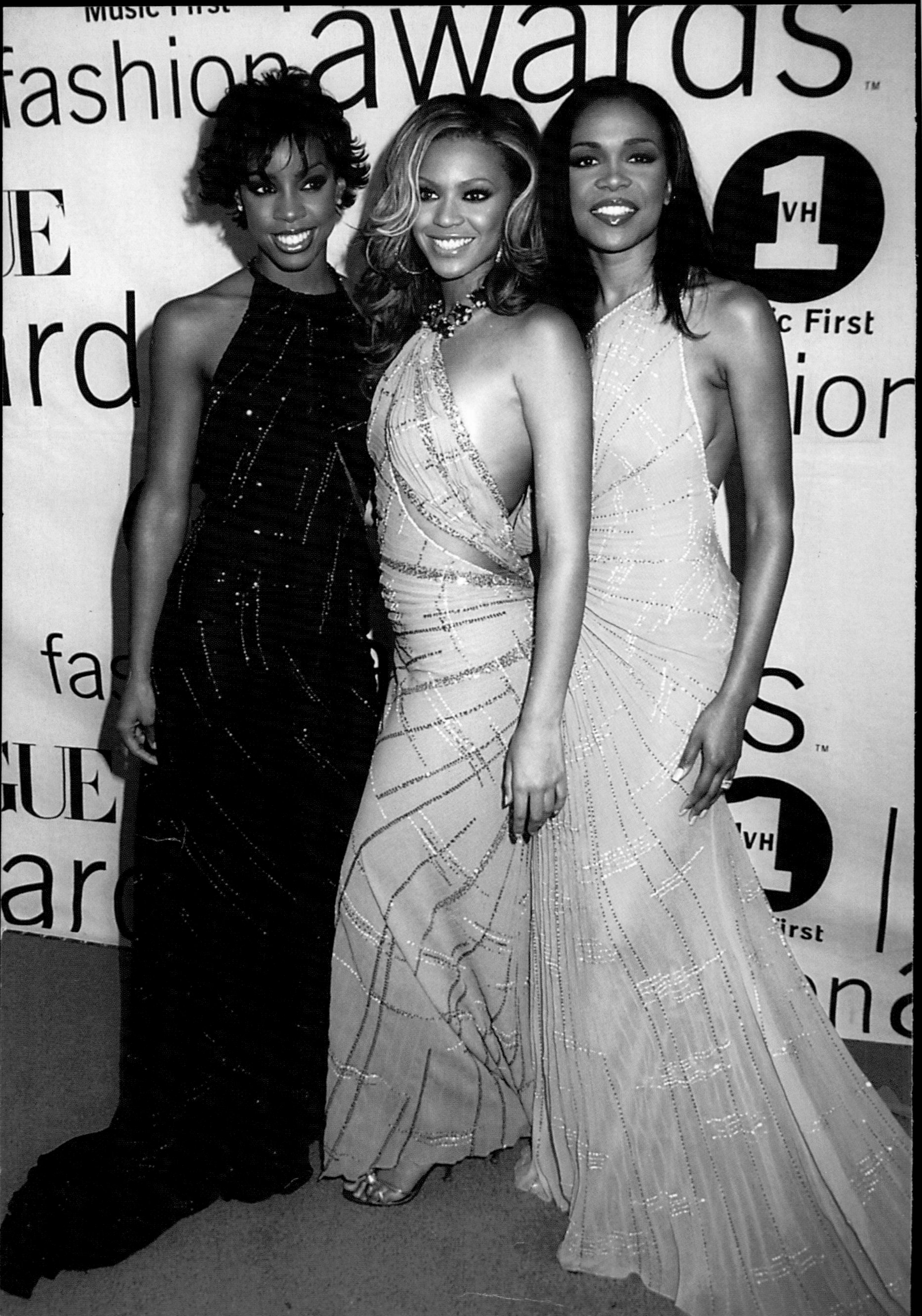

Music First
fashion awards
VH1
Music First
fashion
awards

GALAXY OF SUPERSTARS

Destiny's Child

Dawn FitzGerald

CHELSEA HOUSE PUBLISHERS
Philadelphia

Frontis: Destiny's Child at the VH-1 2000 Fashion Awards. Their mix of flashy style and exciting music have propelled them into superstardom.

CHELSEA HOUSE PUBLISHERS
Editor in Chief: Sally Cheney
Director of Production: Kim Shinners
Creative Manager: Takeshi Takahashi
Manufacturing Manager: Diann Grasse

Staff for DESTINY'S CHILD
Associate Editor: Ben Kim
Picture Researcher: Jane Sanders
Production Assistant: Jaimie Winkler
Series Designer: Takeshi Takahashi
Cover Designer: Terry Mallon
Layout: 21st Century Publishing and Communications, Inc.

The Chelsea House World Wide Web address is
http://www.chelseahouse.com

First Printing

1 3 5 7 9 8 6 4 2

Library of Congress Cataloging-in-Publication Data

Fitzgerald, Dawn.
  Destiny's Child / Dawn Fitzgerald.
    p. cm. — (Galaxy of superstars)
Summary: Profiles the successful singing group that came together at an
audition for pop artists in Houston in 1991 and went on to become the
chart-topping R&B group, Destiny's Child.
Includes bibliographical references (p.   ) and index.
  ISBN 0-7910-6770-X (hardcover)
  1. Destiny's Child (Musical Group)—Juvenile literature. 2. Singers—
United States—Biography—Juvenile literature. [1. Destiny's Child (Musical
Group) 2. Singers. 3. African Americans—Biography. 4. Women—Biography.
5. Rhythm and blues music.] I. Title. II. Series.
ML3930.D43 F57 2002
782.421643'092'2—dc21   2002000365

Dedication: For Sean

Contents

1

THE GRAMMY AWARDS

On February 23, 2000, the 42nd annual Grammy Awards presentation took place at the Los Angeles Staples Center in California. The music industry's highest honor is presented each year in recognition of excellence in the recording arts and sciences. Over 2 billion people, in 180 countries, tuned in that winter evening to watch their favorite artists perform and accept their awards.

Somewhere in the audience sat the beautiful and talented young women of the new R&B (rhythm-and-blues) group Destiny's Child. Although these 19-year-olds were smiling on the outside, on the inside they were in turmoil. They faced a crisis that threatened to destroy their careers as well as friendships that had begun over a decade ago in Houston, Texas.

Destiny's Child was thrilled to have received two Grammy nominations for their second album, *The Writing's on the Wall*, which would eventually sell over 10 million copies worldwide. However, their excitement was tempered by events that had taken place a month earlier. Attending the Grammys as nominated artists should have been the high point of their lives, yet it had turned into a nightmare due to

Although the Grammy nominations for Destiny's Child in 2000 were exciting, there were still inner tensions that threatened to spoil the party for the group. Second from left is Farrah Franklin, who would leave the group in August of 2000 in a bitter parting.

a letter that had been sent by band members LeToya Luckett and LaTavia Roberson.

In the letter, LeToya and LaTavia informed fellow Destiny's Child members, Kelly Rowland and Beyoncé Knowles that they were unhappy with Mathew Knowles managing the group. They demanded separate managers. Later on they would file lawsuits against the group and Mathew.

Unfortunately, there was no simple solution for their complaint. Mathew was lead singer Beyoncé's father, as well as the only father figure Kelly had ever known. He and his wife Tina had struggled to bring Destiny's Child to the level where they were now—Grammy-nominated artists.

At the time of the Grammy Awards, the media was told that due to creative differences LeToya and LaTavia had been replaced. Farrah Franklin and Michelle Williams would join Beyoncé and Kelly as the new Destiny's Child. It would take many months before the entire story was revealed.

As the announcement for the Grammy winner for the best R&B song of the year drew near, there was one question on everyone's mind: Who would appear on stage if Destiny's Child won the award? Would the original members—who recorded the song, but who were no longer part of the group—accept, or would the retooled Destiny's Child take the stage?

Beyoncé told MTV, "We had no idea what was going to happen. We were scared out of our minds. It was the worst thing in life."

Midway through the show when the popular R&B group TLC won in the categories that Destiny's Child had been nominated, the question was irrelevant. Yet, for Kelly and Beyoncé, even more pressing ones remained. Would they be able to survive the departure of two original members? Were the new girls capable of handling the pressure of learning unfamiliar dance routines and songs in a short period of time? But, perhaps the most important question on that disappointing winter evening was something neither Beyoncé nor Kelly had control over. Would the fans continue to support the new Destiny's Child?

2

CHILDHOOD DREAMS

In 1991, 30 eager 10-year-old girls auditioned on stage in Houston, Texas, each of them hoping to be one of the lucky six chosen to form a new pop group called Girls Tyme. After a long day of rehearsals and callbacks, Beyoncé Knowles, Kelly Rowland, and LaTavia Roberson were thrilled to have earned positions in the group that would be managed by Andretta Tillman.

Immediately, Girls Tyme began practicing six hours a day on a variety of R&B, rap, and pop songs, hoping to create their own unique sound. They choreographed dance routines to accompany the songs and began appearing in venues all over the Houston area, including Black Expo, Miss Black Houston Metroplex Pageant, and People's Workshop Sammy Davis Jr. Awards.

The young performers garnered attention and were profiled in the *Houston Chronicle*, where a music critic predicted that they would someday be stars. The expectations were high as Girls Tyme prepared for their first national exposure on the television show *Star Search*. They hoped that a first place win would guarantee their future success in show business. After all, *Star Search* had

---

The trio, as they're now known, actually began as a six-member group of 10-year-old girls. After some setbacks, the group went from six to four. Only Beyoncé Knowles and Kelly Rowland have stuck with Destiny's Child all the way.

helped launch the careers of many entertainers.

Unfortunately, Girls Tyme did not walk away with the first-place trophy. Years later Kelly still recalls the disappointment, "Even when it hurt so bad, we're still smiling, and when we walked offstage everybody just broke down. Imagine ten- or eleven-year-olds just breaking down and crying."

What was supposed to have been their big break, instead turned out to be the first of many small break-ups for the young performers. After failing to win *Star Search*, three of the six members of Girls Tyme left the group. Only Beyoncé, Kelly, and LaTavia remained.

For these three, the *Star Search* loss made them even more determined to succeed. The girls regrouped, adding a fourth member, LeToya Luckett, and gaining a new manager in Beyoncé's father, Mathew Knowles. Now all they needed was a new name to celebrate their renewed commitment.

In the following months the group tried out a few names: Cliché, Something Fresh, the Dolls and Destiny. But nothing seemed to click until Beyoncé's mother Tina, who became the stylist for the group, came across a page marked with the girl's pictures in her bible. In the Book of Isaiah the word "destiny" caught her eye. They added the word "child," and from then on the group was known as Destiny's Child.

Destiny's Child had their work cut out for them. In the early 1990s, boy groups, like New Kids on the Block and Boyz II Men, dominated the pop music scene. The girls knew that they needed to work twice as hard if they hoped to succeed in this highly competitive business.

During the school year, Beyoncé, Kelly, LaTavia, and LeToya attended different schools in the Houston area, but during the summers they attended what Mathew Knowles dubbed "summer camp." Knowles had given up his six-figure income as Xerox's number-one salesman of medical equipment so he could manage Destiny's Child full time.

Summer camp for the young performers consisted of eight hours of singing, dancing, and drills aimed at perfecting their style and establishing cohesiveness as a group. Kelly told the *Miami Herald*, "A lot of people don't have the hunger and patience we did at the age of 10 and 11 years old."

To achieve their goal the girls sacrificed social activities most teenagers engage in, like slumber parties and meeting friends at the mall. Instead, the quartet rehearsed at the Headlines Hair Salon, a beauty shop owned by Beyoncé's mother. There, the girls would try out new routines and songs on a captive audience. Tina Knowles told Jancee Dunn of *Rolling Stone*, "They used to go in and perform, and make the customers sit there. The customers couldn't leave because they were locked under the dryers."

After performances, the girls would some-times receive tips. But Mathew was not interested in monetary compensation at this point in his young protégés career. He focused on tips of a different kind—advice on how the group could improve.

Vernell Jackson, family friend, and present manager of the Headlines Salon, told *Rolling Stone*:

> They were about nine or ten. They would do their routines, and Mathew would ask us to critique: 'Well, what do you think? What needs to be worked on?' And they would start all over again. Beyoncé partic-ularly always had that thing about, 'I want

to do it right,' She wanted to work on it, like her singing and her voice lessons and her dancing. She always wanted to be maybe like Janet Jackson or Michael Jackson— those type of people.

Destiny's Child gained additional singing experience at another important location in Houston—St. John's Methodist Church. The girls sang in the gospel choir every Sunday, as well as attending church services and Sunday school classes. Their religion and faith would play a key role in sustaining them in their drive to succeed in the record business.

By the time the girls reached high school their schedules were so hectic, between schoolwork, practice, and local performances, that their parents hired a tutor to home school them. Even though they were devoted to music, it was clear that a good education was important as well.

When Kelly turned nine, she moved out of her home where she lived with her mother, Doris, and older brother, Orlando, and moved in with Beyoncé's family. Doris, who worked as a nanny, agreed to this arrangement because it made the frequent practice and performances easier for Kelly to attend. It also allowed her to pursue her dream of becoming a star.

Kelly's family visited her on weekends and spoke to her on the phone every day. Not surprisingly though, she considers the Knowles her adopted family. She said in a recent interview, "I call Beyoncé 'My Angel' because of all she's given me, and I trust her dad, because he's my father figure."

Beyoncé and Kelly both agree that having Mathew and Tina as their manager and stylist, respectively, has been beneficial to the group. "There's nobody that can keep you in check

like your mom and your dad," Beyoncé told the *Toronto Sun*. "They'll keep us down to earth. We know that we're just people. We know that all this can be taken away from us."

Under Mathew and Tina's guidance, Destiny's Child gained a strong following in the Houston area. Their impressive vocal harmonies and glamorous image led to opening performances for big name acts like Immature, SWV, and Dru Hill. In 1995 they were signed by Elektra records but were dropped less than a year later.

Though disappointed, the girls never gave up

The original four members of Destiny's Child grew up in the Houston area. They gathered a small following of fans in Texas during the group's early years.

on themselves, and in 1996 they refocused their efforts on completing their first album— this time for the Columbia record label. Beyoncé told *Ebony*, "There would be no Destiny's Child without my father's vision and my mother's support and love and vision. Nobody in the world had confidence and believed in us like my mom and dad."

As they made progress on the album, Destiny's Child had the opportunity to work with some of the best R&B artists in the industry. Vincent Herbert, who had previously produced hits for Brandy and Toni Braxton, handled two of the tracks on the debut album that would be entitled "Destiny's Child."

Dwayne Wiggins of Tony!Toni!Tone! produced 11 of the songs from a studio in Oakland, California. Wiggins told the *Houston Chronicle*, "I immediately knew that these girls were going to be huge. They were just like regular teenagers at times, you know, laughing and playing, which was refreshing to see. But they took their work very seriously."

Work continued on the album and in July 1997, Wycleff Jean came to Houston to do a remix of the song "No, No, No" at Houston's Digital Studios. Before the album's official release Destiny's Child received a fortunate break when the song "Killing Time" appeared on the *Men in Black* soundtrack.

The 1997 film *Men in Black*, starring Will Smith, was a box office hit. Beyoncé, Kelly, LeToya, and LaTavia flew to New York City and appeared with Smith at Tower Records as part of a promotion for *Men In Black*. After the appearance, the quartet attended a party at the restaurant Planet Hollywood that included celebrities Jada Pinkett, Mary J. Blige, and Sean "Puffy" Combs.

The girls were only 16 years old at the time and were amazed at their good fortune. After working together for so many years, it seemed that things were finally starting to happen for them. Little did they realize that with the release of their self-titled debut album, the best was yet to come.

3

DESTINY'S DEBUT

After two years in the making, in February 1998, Destiny's Child released their first album. Almost immediately they began touring all over the country, performing in major cities like New York, Los Angeles, and Chicago. Sometimes the concerts were solo and other times they performed with Wyclef Jean and Boyz II Men. The schedule was always grueling. During some months, the teenage quartet gave as many as 18 back-to-back shows.

As the girls made appearances, signed autographs, and continued singing and dancing, their album climbed the *Billboard* record charts. A few of the singles from the album became hits. The funky dance song "No, No, No" reached the top 10 in both the United States and Great Britain and was followed by "With Me" and "Get on the Bus." The latter appearing on the *Why Do Fools Fall in Love?* soundtrack.

For the teenagers from Houston, Texas, the attention and success they were now experiencing surpassed their childhood dreams. "We've been wanting to sing since we were like two, three, four years old," Kelly told *Teen People* magazine. "So to have a show where you [have] like

Beyoncé Knowles started writing songs for Destiny's Child on their first album. The Knowles family, including live-in honorary member Kelly Rowland, has given Destiny's Child direction right from the start.

20,000 people coming to see you—what more could you ask for?"

Fans were flocking to see the fresh new girls group with the beautiful vocal harmonies and the hip fashion style. "I know we've started a whole fashion thing in music with R&B and pop," Beyoncé told the *Toronto Sun*. "A lot of the pop artists now, they dress up more." Kelly told *Honey* magazine that when it come to clothes, "I'll try anything. Hey, that's how trends are started, right? By one person daring to wear something different."

For all their glamour and glitz, Beyoncé felt that Destiny's Child needed to be based on something more. "I think it is important to look good and to dance," she admitted, "but I think it's more important to be a true artist than a half-talent, because beauty fades. There are millions of beautiful bands that have come and gone, but if you don't have any substance and talent behind it, then after one or two albums there's another beautiful band there to take your place."

Watching the numerous costume changes at a Destiny's Child concert—from army fatigue chic to sequined gowns, to white leather shorts and satin tube tops—it's obvious that the group enjoys dressing up. Dressing up was the easy part. The real challenge came after the shows ended and the girls needed to dress down and remain grounded in their values, community, and commitments to their church and each other.

Having Tina and Mathew's firm hand guiding them along the way certainly helped. In all the interviews that preceded the release of their first album Kelly, Beyoncé, LaTavia, and LeToya were always respectful, polite, and humble. They did not drink, use foul language, or even date

very much—they simply didn't have the time.

Taking time out to visit St. John's United Methodist Church in Houston—even if it meant catching a red-eye flight to be there for Sunday morning services—reminded the girls where they had come from and what was truly important in life.

Pastor Rasmus of St. John's United Methodist Church told Jancee Dunn of *Rolling Stone*:

Costumes for Destiny's Child capture their cutting-edge style. The group's performances flash with impressive sets, scenery, dancing, and the famous Destiny's Child flair.

> The girls grew up here. . . . These girls have always had the desire to do this thing. And Mathew is a very determined guy, so I had few doubts that he was gonna ultimately do it. And I've seen the sacrifices that he and Tina have made to see this happen. And that's one thing I really admire about them—

they're taking no prisoners as it relates to someone messing with their kids. I mean, just because the kids are making money doesn't mean you just release them to the wolves [who] are circling.

Although the wolves may have been circling, the girls were too busy fulfilling their engagements to notice. Besides traveling around the world, singing, and dancing, all four appeared in advertisements for Soft and Beautiful Botanicals hair products. They enjoyed the attention and opportunity to do some modeling.

Despite their busy schedules, Destiny's Child found time to appear at benefits and support worthy causes. In the summer of 1999, the group participated in a New York City fundraiser held by Concept Cure, the WNBA's official cancer charity. The fundraiser was held for WNBA player, Kim Perot, who played for the Houston Comets and had been recently diagnosed with lung cancer. C-Note, Grenique, rapper Cha Cha, and many other performers donated their time and talent to raise money for Kim's treatments.

Destiny's Child was quickly developing a reputation as a hard-working band and the positive response to their first album prompted the group to return to the studio to work on a second. Where the first album took a little over two years to complete, the second would take just two and a half months.

Unfortunately, for the quartet that had performed together since they were 10, fame, hectic schedules, and control issues would begin to exert pressure on the group. While Beyoncé clearly emerged as the group's leader, undercurrents of dissatisfaction appeared.

Contributing to the tension was the unending scrutiny by the media. They analyzed Destiny's

Child's every move and made predictions on whether the young women could survive their sudden fame. As Destiny's Child labored to complete their second album in hopes of proving that they were not just one-album-wonders, many thought that they somehow missed the writing on the wall.

4

THE WRITING'S
ON THE WALL

In June 1999, Destiny's Child released its second album, *The Writing's on the Wall*. Once again, the group worked with top-notch artists in the music industry, including Rodney Jerkins, Missy Elliott, Daryl Simmons, Chad Elliot, and Dwayne Wiggins. Kevin She'kspere Briggs helped produce the hit "Bills, Bills, Bills" which became the number one pop and R&B song in the United States by July. The song was also a smash hit in Europe, making it into the U.K. top 10 as well.

While women immediately identified with the sassy girl-power theme, some men were not as enthusiastic, accusing the group of male-bashing. In "Bills, Bills, Bills" the girls sang about a guy who uses his girlfriend's credit card to buy her expensive gifts, maxing out on the card and taking advantage of the relationship.

The song "Bug A Boo" describes a relationship where an insecure man needs to know his girlfriend's every move. Paging her and keeping tabs on whom she is with and where she is going, he acts more like a stalker than a boyfriend. The video for the track depicts Destiny's Child as four confident females who will not allow themselves to be ruled by men who act like a "bug a boo."

Their second album, *The Writings on the Wall*, earned Destiny's Child a coveted Grammy Award for the single "Say My Name." But turmoil was to follow soon as original members LaTavia Luckett and LeToya Roberson quit the band and were replaced by Farrah Franklin and Michelle Williams (pictured here). Of the new members, only Michelle would stay on to complete the lineup of today.

The biggest hit from the *The Writing's on the Wall* was the Grammy-winning, "Say My Name." In this song, a woman is having a conversation with her boyfriend over the telephone and she begins to suspect that he is unfaithful to her. Suspicious that another girlfriend is in the room, she asks her boyfriend to "say my name." He refuses, so she ends the relationship rather than play games with a cheater.

Judging from the phenomenal success of *The Writing's on the Wall*, the album ultimately appealed to both males and females with its empowering message, soaring harmonies, and strong dance rhythms. It spent 47 weeks in the U.S. top 40 and eventually went multi-platinum. According to Soundscan, 5.8 million copies were sold in the U.S. with a total of 10 million in sales worldwide.

Destiny's Child had finally reached the mega-stardom they had worked so hard for. The girls were especially proud of their second album because of their increased creative input throughout the production process. Beyoncé took on a greater songwriting role, in addition to handling most of the lead vocals. She also received production credit on most of the songs on the album.

Beyoncé explained her songwriting dilemma in a recent interview. "I battle all the time with writing a commercial song over one that's really special to me," she explained. "The ultimate for me would be to write a song that becomes important and really moves people and makes them think, like 'What's Going On' by Marvin Gaye."

As Beyoncé emerged as the leader of the quartet, control issues surfaced among the group members that threatened to split Destiny's Child in two. In December 1999, LaTavia Luckett and LeToya Roberson delivered letters to Mathew Knowles stating that he was not their manager anymore. According to Christopher Farley of *Time*, they also filed a lawsuit against Mathew "charging that his 'greed, insistence on control, self-dealing and promotion of his daughter's interests at the expense of Plaintiffs, became the dominant forces in Destiny's Child.'"

Unfortunately, the letter could not have come at a more inopportune time. At the close of 1999, the group had two hit singles on the chart and a platinum-selling album. They were in the midst of touring and promotions with the end of the year music award shows about to begin, including the prestigious Grammy Awards for which they had received two nominations. In addition, Destiny's Child was also nominated for an NAACP Image Award and a Lady Soul Train Music Award.

Many groups before them had faced the departure of members with disastrous results. The Spice Girls went from a quintet to a quartet and have not been heard from since. En Vogue began as a quartet and then lost one of its members as well as its audience when it continued on as a trio. All this weighed heavily on Beyoncé and Kelly as they pondered the demands in the letter.

If the letter's accusations were simply a matter of control and favoritism, then possibly the group may have been able to arrive at an amicable agreement. But, according to an interview with MTV, LeToya and LaTavia also accused Mathew of greed, stating, "despite his lack of [music business] experience, [he] also insisted on compensation terms far more favorable to him than those usually available in the industry."

Mathew responded to MTV, "I think that the real truth will come out of the court proceedings. I can very clearly say that there [has] been no misappropriation of funds and that two members of the group, the background singers LeToya and LaTavia, decided to fire the manager of Destiny's Child without discussing it with the other members, Beyoncé and Kelly, the lead and second lead singers."

After the dust had settled from their tumultuous 2000, the trio of Michelle, Beyoncé and Kelly emerged stronger than ever as the new Destiny's Child.

Beyoncé and Kelly now needed to make one of the most difficult decisions of their life concerning the future of the band. While part of them desperately wanted to hold the group together, in their hearts they knew that the rift was deep and the accusations very serious.

According to Lynn Norment of *Ebony*, the girls sought guidance from their pastor and prayed a lot. "We went on a praying week," Beyoncé told Norment. "We just prayed, prayed, prayed. We said, 'God, we are not trying to put a time limit on you, but we are asking you what to do. If you send two new members to us, then that is what we will do. If not, then we know that you want Kelly and me to just finish out (promoting) the album.' "

In January 2000, their prayers were answered. Destiny's Child issued a brief statement to the media stating that due to creative differences, LeToya and LaTavia had left the group and would be replaced by Farrah Franklin of Los Angeles, California, and Michelle Williams of Rockford, Illinois.

Farrah and Michelle were no strangers to Destiny's Child. Farrah had been one of the background dancers on the "Bills, Bills, Bills" video, and Michelle had met the band members when she had toured as a background singer for Monica. The new additions to the group brought beauty, dancing, and singing ability, as well as the added bonus of being the same age as Kelly and Beyoncé. It appeared to be a perfect fit.

Immediately, Farrah and Michelle needed to step in and replace the departing members, who had worked together as a group for close to a decade. There was enormous pressure to achieve a seamless transition. The retooled Destiny's Child, now sometimes referred to in print as DC, practiced 12 hours a day, seven days a week.

Farrah and Michelle learned song and dance routines in a matter of weeks in order to fulfill commitments made prior to the break-up. Beyoncé told *Ebony*, "They definitely were angels sent from God. It took a lot of hard work. There were struggles and tears and sweat, but we got through it."

Meanwhile, LeToya and LaTavia began working with Jagged Edge twin brothers Brian and Brandon Casey on demo material in Atlanta. Jagged Edge and Destiny's Child once toured together. With Brian and Brandon's help in songwriting and producing, the ex-Destiny's Child members hoped to form their own successful band. They planned on calling the group Angel and focusing on danceable R&B music.

As LaTavia and LeToya formed a new group,

their old bandmates prepared for their first appearance without them. The remodeled Destiny's Child performed at the NBA All-Star game in Oakland, California, as well as the Soul Train Music Awards. Beyoncé told *Ebony*, "There is nothing harder than performing for a room full of celebrities."

Fortunately all their hard work paid off and the new Destiny's Child passed these first critical tests. Now, the question was, could the new girls hold up under the pressure? The answer came five months later in August, when Farrah Franklin abruptly left the group.

The remaining new member, Michelle Williams explained Farrah's sudden departure.

A group cannot work when you have people whose mission isn't the same. Everybody's got to want the same thing to go places, and everyone has to want to work. This group works hard. . . . Everyone has to know her role in the group. Our manager likes to tell us when Michael Jordan was playing ball, they threw the ball to him because they knew he would make the points. Everyone knows her role now, and that's what makes the organization run smoothly.

Beyoncé put it bluntly in an interview with *Time*. "She didn't come to work for two weeks," she said of Farrah. "She couldn't handle it. And so she had to go."

Like departing band members before her, Farrah made plans to continue in the music business. She told MTV about her five-month stint as a member of Destiny's Child, "I felt like I had no say in which way my career was going, and I lost my identity."

Throughout this transition period, Kelly and Beyoncé tried to remain calm, positive, and focused on their work. They showed maturity in continuing to move forward and refraining from making negative comments to the press no matter how critical the

media became of the group's revolving-door line up.

Beyoncé told *Ebony*, "One of the reasons that the transition went so smoothly is because Kelly and I refused to speak negatively. We didn't even defend ourselves, and there were so many lies and rumors going around. We didn't go on a rampage, though we had good reason to. But what would have been the point? I'm just glad the fans stuck with us."

Kelly looked on the bright side of the situation, saying "Just keep giving them something to talk about, 'cause that'll just sell an extra 100,000 records that week."

In fact, Destiny's Child was hotter than ever. All the press the girls received gained them greater attention and exposed more people to their music. Beyoncé explained their continuing popularity to *Entertainment Weekly*, "We have the talent to back up all the drama. If we were weak [musically] then people would have said, 'Man, they have too much drama.' But when we get up on the stage and we sing and perform, that's the thing that really matters."

The slim and trim trio worked great as a threesome. The group became more popular and performed for charities, sporting events, and on television. Destiny's Child performed at the lighting of the New York City Christmas tree in 2000.

Kelly commented in an interview, "We tried to help Farrah but I guess the business was too much for her. But she was disloyal to our fans because she stood them up, and that's something Destiny's Child does not do."

After Farrah's departure, Destiny's Child decided to remain a trio, making it difficult for critics to resist the Diana Ross and the Supremes comparisons. Still, Beyoncé took the high road, telling *Time* magazine, "I love and respect the Supremes because they were glamorous, and whenever they walked into a room they lit up the room. That's what Destiny's Child tries to do."

In the 1960s, the Supremes were one of the most successful Motown groups. The talented trio consisting of Diana Ross, Mary Wilson, and Florence Ballard originally began as a quartet in the late 1950s in Detroit, Michigan. Their first number one hit was "Where Did Our Love Go?" and it was quickly followed by four consecutive number one hits in 1964-65 ("Baby Love," "Stop! In the Name of Love," "Come See About Me," and "Back in My Arms Again"). But behind the scenes of their phenomenal success were bitter battles for control, as Diana Ross, with the support of Motown President Berry Gordy, stepped out as lead vocalist in the group.

Ross eventually left the Supremes to pursue a solo career and make movies. Although the group continued on into the early 1970s, the Supremes never recaptured the stardom they had experienced earlier in their careers.

Now, rumors were flying about the future of Destiny's Child, and some in the entertainment industry made unflattering parallels between Beyoncé and Diana Ross. Would Destiny's Child break up at the height of their success? In 1999, many critics predicted that the end was certainly near. Many of them joked that the group was like the reality television show, *Survivor*—you never knew

who was going to be voted out of the band next.

Michelle said in an interview during this stressful time, "There's always gonna be negative people pulling you down. It's a shame people would rather pull you down than lift you up. If you lift someone up, before you know it you're lifted too."

However, it was Beyoncé more than the others who took the negative comments to heart. After all, they were criticizing her parents, calling them controlling and saying that they were using Destiny's Child as a vehicle to catapult their daughter's solo career.

Beyoncé resolved to use all the negativity and ridicule, channeling it into creative fire in the recording studio where Destiny's Child had returned to work on their third album. She was determined to silence the critics and to prove beyond a doubt that she and Destiny's Child would not only survive the past year's controversy, but emerge as stronger independent women in the process.

Destiny's Child accept their awards for best R&B performance by a duo or group at the 43rd annual Grammy Awards. Finally receiving recognition after years of struggle and accusations by ex-members, the trio were on a roll towards even bigger success.

SURVIVING
AND THRIVING

On February 13, 2001, Destiny's Child released its third album, which was appropriately entitled *Survivor*. Beyoncé co-produced and wrote most of the album herself and clearly emerged as a strong creative force. But *Survivor* also goes a long way in showcasing the talents of Kelly Rowland and Michelle Williams. It is not simply an album focused on Beyoncé's talents, even though she alone played the major role in directing its content and style.

In an interview with *Teen People*, Beyoncé described the differences between this new album compared to the previous two. "Destiny's Child is such a strong group now," she said, "as far as our relationships with each other. . . . Everyone sings lead on almost every song, and I produced and wrote every song on the album, and I made sure that you could hear Michelle and Kelly because they have beautiful voices."

When asked where she got the idea for the title of the new album, Beyoncé admits that she was getting tired of hearing all the jokes on the radio that went like this: How is Destiny's Child like the reality-based television show, *Survivor*? You never know who's going to get kicked out of the band next. "It was creative, it was clever," she told Evelyn McDonnell of the

---

Praise and recognition rained down on Destiny's Child upon the release of their third album. Hasbro created dolls in the likeness of the popular singers.

Miami Herald. "But I was like, 'If I hear one more joke'. . . . I'm happy that that mean radio station said that little funky comment, because it inspired a song. Got anything else to say?"

The song "Survivor" may be the first break-up song in history to contain the lyrics "I'm not going to dis you on the Internet/'Cause my mother taught me better than that." Michelle felt that the song was a hit because it means different things to different people. "A lot of people thought Destiny's Child wouldn't make it after its member changes," she said. "But the song's about surviving other things. We've got so many friends who've survived death of close friends, lost jobs, breast cancer, and all kinds of things. We incorporated that into the song. Everyone on the face of the Earth has survived something."

Kelly was just thankful to have survived the video shoot for the song "Survivor." In the video, the girls are dressed in skimpy native attire as they appear to face the challenges of a tropical island, aping the appearance of the television show *Survivor.* In reality, they spent the entire shoot shivering on an unseasonably cold day in Malibu, California—so one can certainly add acting ability to the list of Destiny's Child's talents.

In their previous two albums, Destiny's Child had been accused of male-bashing. In light of this, Beyoncé tried to write about more universal themes for *Survivor.* Michelle praised Beyoncé's songwriting skills in an interview with the *Chicago Tribune.* "Beyoncé has truly been an inspiration. She wrote 'Survivor' in five minutes. That's something that would've taken me six months or a year to do. It's good to be with someone who does a way better job than I ever could."

Of her own songwriting, Kelly simply stated, "I have gifts that I can share with the world. Writing songs is not one of them." More important to Kelly than the source of the lyrics was the fact that this album, recorded after the break ups and the scathing remarks of critics, proved that Destiny's Child could come together in the studio and support one another. Kelly admitted in a recent interview that generosity is very much a part of her nature. "I'm a very giving person—that's just my spirit, an unconscious thing. I look out for other people, sometimes even before I look after myself."

Besides having a giving nature, Kelly is best described as the rebel of the group, an independent woman who is not waiting around for a boyfriend to give her diamonds. Instead, she

The Destiny's Child song "Independent Woman Part 1" appeared on the soundtrack for the film *Charlie's Angels* and was number one for 11 weeks. Here the girls perform at the Brit Awards in London and adopt a *Charlie's Angels*-like pose.

goes out and buys them for herself. It's no surprise that the song "Independent Women Part I" wound up as the first song on the album.

What was surprising was the phenomenal success of the song as it climbed the charts to number one. The song "Independent Women Part I" appeared on the soundtrack for the 2000 film, *Charlie's Angels*, starring Lucy Liu, Cameron Diaz, and Drew Barrymore. The song was number one for 11 weeks. The only other single from a soundtrack to hold the number one spot longer was Whitney Houston's "I Will Always Love You."

Another popular song on the album, "Bootylicious," is "full of busy, skitter-skatter beats, with strong vocals providing the forward motion," according to music critic Rob Sheffield of *Rolling Stone*. Sheffield especially liked the part of the song that "flips the guitar riff from Stevie Nicks's song 'Edge of Seventeen' to the chant 'I shake my jelly at every chance/When I whip with my hips you step into a trance.'"

Beyoncé wrote the song "Bootylicious" while on a long plane flight to London, England, for a performance. She told MTV, "We were bored [on] this long flight to London, and I was like, 'You know what, I gotta do something.' I'd listened to this Stevie Nicks track ["Edge of Seventeen"] and I'm like, 'This is hot!' and the word "Bootylicious" just popped in my head. . . . The meaning of the song is just confidence. . . . It's all about attitude and feeling good about yourself and not looking like everybody on TV."

On May 6, 2001, Beyoncé, Kelly, and Michelle decided to appear on television. Displaying their sense of humor, the trio made an appearance on the comedy show *Saturday Night Live*. For months prior to their appearance on the show, *Saturday Night Live* had been doing a parody of Destiny's Child called the Gemini Twins. The

skit featured the girls as divas, snapping their fingers and satirizing the revolving-door line up of the group.

They had a great time on the show working with guest host Pierce Bronsan and meeting Stevie Nicks, formerly of the group Fleetwood Mac. Coincidentally, while Destiny's Child was rehearsing in the NBC studios for *Saturday Night Live*, Nicks was in a nearby studio as a guest on the *Rosie O'Donnell Show*. The trio met her there and asked her to be in the "Bootylicious" video, since it was inspired by one of Nick's songs. Nicks wound up juggling a few appointments and appeared in the video. Because they were fans of Fleetwood Mac, Beyoncé, Kelly, and Michelle were thrilled to meet her. Michelle described the video shoot to Colin Devenish of *LiveDaily*, saying, "She gave us personalized CDs, and she wrote letters to

Destiny's Child won "Choice Pop Group" at the 2001 Teen Choice Awards, one of the many accolades that they would win that year.

all three of us. She was saying, 'Stay like you are and don't change,' and she basically let us know how not to get consumed in the business. 'Even though you're in it, don't let it take away your life.'"

Destiny's Child incorporated a song from one other artist on the *Survivor* album. Earlier in the year Mathew Knowles had given the girls a copy of the Bee Gees song "Emotion," which was a hit for Samantha Sang in 1978. At first the girls were a little intimidated. They wanted to do justice to the song, so Beyoncé went into the studio and rearranged "Emotion," complete with handclaps and acoustic guitars, in order to showcase the trios' vocal talents. Everything came together beautifully on the album and Destiny's Child hopes that someday they will have the opportunity to perform the song with the Bee Gees.

One of the more unusual songs on the album is "The Story of Beauty," which deals with the topic of domestic violence and abuse. During their 2001 concert tour for *Survivor*, video screens behind the singers were emblazoned with the message "Never Be Afraid to Tell" while Destiny's Child sang the song. Beyoncé told MTV, "The 'Story of Beauty'. . . . is a pretty controversial yet realistic song that deals with something that happens in most families that no one wants to talk about."

One thing fans were talking about was the success of *Survivor*. Within one week of its debut on May 1, 2001, the album sold over 663,000 copies in the United States alone. *Survivor* skyrocketed to the top of the charts and set a record for selling more copies in one week than any other album by a female group in the last 10 years.

In an interview with the *Miami Herald*, Kelly

credits Beyoncé for her growth as a singer and the new album's success. "On this album I've grown, I sang a lot more of the leads, thanks to Beyoncé," Kelly said, "because I know no other producer would have taken the time and the patience to work with me. In my eyes she's one of the best producers out there."

Even after the incredible success of *Survivor*, Destiny's Child did not take a break or slow their momentum. They appeared at the White House for an inaugural concert celebrating America's youth, where they sang "Independent Women" and "Jumpin' Jumpin'." Beyoncé got up on stage and called out to the audience, "I wanna hear you say Bush!"

They also continued to do what they loved best—touring. To satisfy their legions of fans, they took their popular songs and dance routines on the road for one of their most ambitious tours yet—MTV's *Total Request Live*.

Destiny's Child's popularity led to an invitation to perform at the halftime show during Game 4 of the NBA Finals between the Los Angeles Lakers and the Philadelphia 76ers.

6

ON THE ROAD

Touring is never easy. Living out of a bus, being far away from home, friends, and family can test anyone's endurance and commitment. But for Destiny's Child, the sacrifices of being on the road were well worth the rewards of meeting their fans and performing hit songs from their albums. The MTV inaugural *Total Request Live* Tour kicked off in mid-July 2001. Destiny's Child was the headlining act and appeared with other artists including Nelly, Eve, Jessica Simpson, Dream, and 3LW.

The tour began in Albany, New York, on July 18th and ended two months, 30 cities, and 42 concerts later in Honolulu, Hawaii. In between, the band crossed the United States from Philadelphia to Phoenix, from Seattle to Cincinnati. There was one state, however, where Destiny's Child refused to perform. In South Carolina the state capitol building flies the Confederate flag and in the past has refused to recognize the Martin Luther King Jr. holiday. Destiny's Child, along with other artists and even some professional sports teams, decided to boycott performing in South Carolina in protest against a flag that for many is a symbol of racism.

Touring takes a physical toll on a group as well. Kelly can

For MTV's *Total Request Live* tour, Destiny's Child packed up its action-packed show and took to the road.

attest to that when she recalls how she broke two toes during a backstage accident when the group toured with Christina Aguilera in the fall of 2000. Kelly was struggling with a quick costume change in the dark backstage at Denver's Magness Arena when she fell over a ramp and broke the second and third toes on her right foot.

However, she did not let the accident slow her down. Donning a sparkly white brace on her right foot, she continued to tour and performed most of her songs while sitting on a stool. Beyoncé's 14-year-old sister Solange stepped in to perform all of the dance moves with the group until Kelly recovered. Beyoncé told *Teen People*, "For a long time, I was on the road without my sister, so I felt like I was missing out. She was becoming a young lady, and I did not see her for years and years and years, so it is such a blessing to see my sister grow and to go on the road with her."

Destiny's Child was thankful that everyone was healthy for the MTV *Total Request Live* Tour. They were determined to give their loyal fans a concert they would never forget. Judging from the reviews and sold-out tickets across the country, they succeeded beyond their expectations.

From the moment they hit the stage, Beyoncé, Kelly, and Michelle were in total command of the audience. The set was a stage within a stage, with three huge video monitors at the back for close-ups of the group. The girls wore flashy, sequined outfits and changed costumes numerous times throughout the concert in keeping with their fashion trend status. During wardrobe changes, recorded interviews played on the large screens that showed the trio talking about what inspired them to write the songs. Male and female dancers performed hip-hop choreographed moves for the majority of the songs, giving the

concert a more polished feel than previous tours.

Destiny's Child opened the concert with one of their biggest hits, the Grammy-winning "Say My Name." Choosing to begin with their top song showed confidence in their ability to hold the audience's attention. Most bands save their biggest hit for later in a concert. Destiny's Child, on the other hand, came out and put it all on the line right from the beginning.

They sang renditions of "Bootylicious" and merged "Jumpin' Jumpin'" with a campy Tina Turner-esque sendup of Credence Clearwater Revival's "Proud Mary." The girls continued their energetic performance with "Nasty Girl," a song many critics find ironic. Lorraine Ali of *Newsweek* wrote, "And while they sing about 'nasty girls' who should 'put some clothes on,'

Destiny's Child has endured criticism of its choice of clothing and its impact on younger audiences, but the group claims that it is "sexy" rather than "nasty," the kind of style they put down in their own song "Nasty Girl."

they never seem to be wearing more than a wash-cloth's worth of material between them."

In an interview with the *Toronto Sun*, Beyoncé explains the distinction between nasty and sexy, saying, "We definitely consider ourselves role models. . . . We're very aware there are people looking up to us. But there's a line between sexy and nasty, and Destiny's Child is sexy, yes we are, but we're never nasty."

Beyoncé told Maria Neuman of *Honey*, "With everything that's been written about me and all the preconceived notions, people expect this diva. Well, I'm not Diana Ross. I actually think of myself as a pretty shy person, I'm low mainte-nance and I can honestly say I have never done anything negative to anybody. It's almost like people *want* me to be something I'm not."

Beyoncé's vocal gymnastics throughout the concert showcased what she is—a very talented singer. Wearing a white satin sarong, Beyoncé is in the solo spotlight for a version of "Dangerously in Love," for which she received a standing ovation night after night.

An a cappella gospel melody midway through the show silenced the few critics who have claimed that the group's vocal talents are less than stellar. Beyoncé arranged the gospel number, which featured "You've Been So Good" (also written by Beyoncé) as well as the trio's versions of Kirk Franklin's "Now Behold the Lamb" and Richard Smallwood's "Total Praise." The pre-dominately teen audience was still as they listened to the sweet harmonies. Beyoncé told *Newsweek* magazine, "I just know that God is on our side, because we conquered things we thought we weren't never gonna overcome."

Destiny's Child's message of overcoming life's setbacks hit home with the final two songs on the concert, "Survivor" and "Happy Face." As

Beyoncé, Kelly, and Michelle sang and danced around the stage waving away balloons and confetti, the audience was on its feet singing along with them. Michelle told Colin Devenish of *LiveDaily*, "That's what's so cool about our shows. Everybody knows all the songs."

What everyone doesn't always know is how important giving back to the community is to the members of Destiny's Child. Kelly and Beyoncé in particular have never forgotten the needs of their hometown in Houston, Texas. Recently, they contributed $500,000 dollars to build a recreational facility for area youth. The girls along with manager, Mathew Knowles, presented the donation to Pastor Rudy Rasmus of St. John's United Methodist Church. The church will use the money to build the center, which will be named the Center for Youth at St. John's Downtown.

When not lending monetary support to worthy causes, the members of Destiny's Child do not hesitate to lend their time and celebrity to help educate and inform people. A good example of this type of volunteerism is the band's involvement with Levi-Strauss and MTV's Fight for Your Rights Charities, which aim to take a stand against discrimination. From August 15 through September 6, 2001, Levi's donated 100 percent of the proceeds from its hottest-selling Levi's jeans to the anti-discrimination charities.

Levi's, MTV, and Destiny's Child want to encourage and empower young people to fight prejudice in their own communities. Beyoncé said in an interview, "We're excited to team up with Levi's and MTV's 'Fight For Your Rights' campaign because we feel we can help spread the word among teens about how they can get involved in fighting discrimination. Young people are smart shoppers. We want to give them ways

Not only did 2001 see Destiny's Child winning a stunning amount of awards but also their most visible commitment yet to charities and other notable causes, including building and renovation projects in Houston and the Fight For Your Rights charities.

to take a stand on this issue and let them know that they can purchase with a purpose."

At this point in their successful careers, Destiny's Child was searching for their purpose, both individually and as a group. With three hit albums, numerous awards, spokesperson contracts with Target, AT&T, and L'Oreál, and thousands of concert appearances in their past, the band looked to the future with the hopes of pursuing solo projects while still remaining together as Destiny's Child.

7

INDEPENDENT
WOMEN

Contrary to the predictions, Kelly was the first to break out in a solo project of her own. Since Beyoncé received greater attention as lead singer in Destiny's Child's first two albums, people assumed that she would be the first to record without the other members of the group. Kelly told *Honey*, "People assume I'm just here because of Beyoncé. It irritates me, like they're not appreciating my talent."

Kelly proved she has plenty of talent of her own when she recorded a song entitled "Angel" for the Chris Rock movie *Down to Earth*. The film is a 2001 remake of the 1941 movie *Here Comes Mr. Jordan*, which was also remade in 1978 as *Heaven Can Wait* with Warren Beatty. The soundtrack, which was released in February 2001, also featured songs by Monica, Jill Scott, Ruff Endz, and Jagged Edge.

Working on the song "Angel" inspired Kelly to want to record a solo album in the future. In addition, she hopes to try some acting as well. "I'd love to do a *Waiting to Exhale* kind of movie or a teeny-bopper movie, because I'm a big teeny-bopper movie freak," she said.

Although Kelly earned the distinction of being the first Destiny's Child member to branch out musically, Beyoncé—

Many thought Beyoncé Knowles would be the first DC member to branch out into solo projects. But, Kelly Rowland was the first. She worked on a solo song for the Chris Rock movie *Down to Earth*.

with encouragement from her band mates—was the first to try acting. Kelly told the *Sunday Mail*, "When Beyoncé was offered the main part in MTV's remake of *Carmen Jones*, she wasn't sure if she wanted to do it. But Michelle and I knew she should do it, so we made her."

The made-for-television movie *Carmen: A Hip Hopera* is a modern retelling of the 19th century opera *Carmen* by French composer Georges Bizet. According to David Basham of MTV, the film is set in Philadelphia and focuses on the tragic romance between police Sgt. Derrick Hill, played by Mekhi Phifer, and Carmen Brown, played by Beyoncé.

Critics thought that Robert Townsend's casting of Beyoncé as Carmen was a shrewd choice. Evelyn McDonnell of the *Miami Herald* wrote, "On May 8, [2001], Knowles finally busts her much-anticipated solo move. When she makes her entrance as the femme-fatale title character in MTV's *Carmen: A Hip Hopera*, all heads turn to her voluptuous form. Even the haters can't take their eyes off her. Carmen is despicable and irresistible. . . . The demonization of women like Carmen and Knowles is even older than Shakespeare and opera."

According to MTV, this isn't the first time the 1875 opera has been updated with a black cast. In 1943, Oscar Hammerstein II created a Broadway musical by writing English lyrics to accompany Bizet's music for "Carmen Jones." Then in 1954, the legendary Dorothy Dandridge and Harry Belafonte starred in the Oscar-nominated film based on the opera.

Beyoncé was happy to work with fellow artists in the cast, including Mos Def, Lil'Boww Wow, Jermaine Dupri, Wyclef Jean, and Rah Digga. Other actors in the film included Troy Winbrush, Sam Sarpong, Regan Gomez-Peterson, and Joy

Bryant. Not only did Beyoncé have a lot of fun interacting on the set of *Carmen*, but she also proved that she had acting talent.

One critic wrote, "Knowles deserves to emerge from the pack. She has a deep throbbing voice, a knack for catchphrases connected to rhythmic hooks, and beauty by the bucket-load. She's the rare female artist confident enough to assert herself in the studio. And in *Carmen* she proves she can act."

According to *Teen People*, when the film debuted on MTV, Kelly and Michelle were more excited about Beyoncé's performance than she was herself. Kelly said of *Carmen*, "It's so deep that Michelle and I watched it and just went, 'Whoa!'"

With two individual projects under their belts, Destiny's Child members are taking a break from the group and are in the planning process of working on solo albums which will be released at the same time in 2002. Each singer will concentrate on a different share of the market. Kelly's sound will be alternative R&B. Michelle's album will also concentrate on R&B but with an emphasis on gospel, while Beyoncé plans on sticking with pop/R&B, the very music that Destiny's Child has made so successful. The members insist that there will be no competition between them. As strong as they are individually, it will only help to make them that much stronger when they come together to record as a group.

Coming together to support each other, as well as others in need, is becoming a trademark of this band. Destiny's Child joined the ranks of many other popular musicians, including Bruce Springsteen, Aerosmith, Shania Twain, and Jewel, when they appeared recently at the Greater Boston Food Bank to help raise money to help stop hunger. The artists signed autographs for hundreds of fans

Success has taken Destiny's Child around the world on tour and for charity work. While in London, England, the group met Britain's Prince Charles.

who donated canned goods and cash.

Catherine D'Amato, president and CEO of the Greater Boston Food Bank, told *Business Wire*, "It's wonderful that, despite their hectic concert tour schedule, Destiny's Child still makes the time to give back to the hungry in the communities in which they perform. It's also great to see fans supporting the Greater Boston Food bank while enjoying their favorite music."

Besides the problem of hunger, Destiny's Child recently joined the fight for yet another cause—teen pregnancy. Sarah Brown of the National Campaign to Prevent Teen Pregnancy notes, "Despite recent declines, the United States still has the highest teen pregnancy rate in the industrialized world. Four out of 10 girls get pregnant at least once by age 20."

In order to raise awareness of the problem, Destiny's Child—along with 'N Sync, 98°, and Macy Gray—performed on June 5, 2001, at New Jersey's Giants Stadium to launch the Candie's

Foundation. The foundation hopes to raise $500,000 to help prevent teen pregnancy. During the concert they aired several public service announcements, featuring celebrities such as Carmen Electra and Andy Dick encouraging kids to say no to sex.

Beyoncé feels that it is important for celebrities to use their visibility to encourage teenagers to make smart choices. "It's cool to be different from everybody else," she said in a recent interview. "It's cool to wait, it's cool to say no, and we want to let people know that that's how we feel. I know when you look up to certain artists and certain people, and they say it, then you feel like 'OK, it's cool.'"

Along with the concert and public service announcements, all the artists agreed to do teen pregnancy prevention ads. These public service ads are scheduled to run in magazines favored by teens including *Teen People, YM, Cosmogirl,* and *Honey*. But the irony in this is unavoidable according to Dr. Susan Villani, a psychiatrist with the Kennedy Krieger Institute in Baltimore. In many of these magazines, as well as pop culture in general, Dr. Villani reports that "The amount of sexual content has dramatically gone up in the last decade. . . . the difference is, a generation ago it might have been aimed at 15- or 16-year-old girls, and now it's 8- or 10-year old girls."

Unfortunately, teens may be receiving a mixed message. Marketers know that sex sells, and that kids between 9-13 years of age spend money and influence how their parents spend money—to the tune of $170 billion a year, according to a recent National Public Radio report. Although young girls may read pregnancy prevention ads featuring their favorite pop music stars, music and popular culture gives them an entirely different message about sex.

When the self-proclaimed King of Pop, Michael Jackson launched his long-awaited comeback for his 30th anniversary celebration on September 7, 2001, Destiny's Child joined a star-studded line up at New York's Madison Square Garden for the festivities. Jackson's promoter David Gest told MTV prior to the event that "Michael is a huge fan of the pop supergroup and is very excited that Beyoncé, Kelly, and Michelle will perform."

The anniversary celebration lasted nearly five hours and included the Jackson 5/Jacksons reunion, where Michael and his brothers sang a set of his own and the group's past hits. Well-known performers did their renditions of Jackson's classics. Ray Charles and Marc Anthony performed "She's Out of My Life." Whitney Houston sang "Wanna Be Startin' Something," the group 'N Sync joined the Jacksons for "Dance Machine," while Britney Spears teamed with Michael to sing "The Way You Make Me Feel."

Meanwhile, Destiny's Child performed "Bootylicious." Beyoncé told *E! News Daily* as she arrived at the Michael Jackson anniversary celebration, "He's been a huge influence on all of us—especially on 'Bootylicious.' I had him in mind when I wrote the song."

On a more somber note, Michael Jackson and Destiny's Child will team on a song of an entirely different nature in the near future. After terrorist attacks on the World Trade Center, Washington D.C., and Pennsylvania on September 11, 2001, Jackson coordinated fundraising efforts around a new song he wrote, "What More Can I Give." With the help of Destiny's Child and other performers, he hopes to raise more than $50 million for the survivors and families of victims.

Sixteen years ago Jackson helped organize the USA for Africa effort with the song "We Are

the World." Jackson said in a recent interview, "There is a tremendous need for relief dollars right now and through this effort each one of us can play an immediate role in helping comfort so many people."

As for the future, Destiny's Child plans on continuing to work hard. Their last album was a Christmas album with many traditional songs like "Away in the Manger" and "Silent Night," as well as a few originals that Beyoncé wrote.

An NBC Christmas special starring Destiny's Child aired during the holidays as well. The St. John Methodist Church Choir from Houston, Texas—the same choir that Beyoncé and Kelly began singing with when they were nine-year-olds—appeared on the show.

The girls have come a long way since then. Beyoncé told the *Toronto Sun*, "People tell us what we've accomplished but we don't really think about it. It's a blessing and it's very flattering. . . ."

Following the terrorist attacks on the World Trade Center on September 11, 2001, Destiny's Child donated time to fundraise for the victims and survivors. Here they sing in the "Concert for New York" at Madison Square Garden in October 2001.

Their manager, Mathew Knowles, hopes the girls realize their dreams and find happiness and success. He told *Ebony*, "Five years from now, I'd like for them to have happiness and financial freedom. I can see them in movies and doing separate solo projects."

As for the present, Beyoncé, Kelly, and Michelle are enjoying every moment of being a part of one of the most successful girl groups in the world. Beyoncé describes it this way, "When I perform, that's the happiest point I can be at in my life. . . . There is nothing that compares to that joy, especially when you look to your right and to your left and you see these ladies. It is beautiful."

CHRONOLOGY

1992   Girls Tyme appears on the nationally televised talent show *Star Search* and loses; Mathew Knowles becomes the manager for the pop/R&B group, and they change their name to Destiny's Child; original four members are Beyoncé Knowles, Kelly Rowland, LaTavia Roberson, and LeToya Luckett; Tina Knowles becomes the group's stylist.

1995   Signed and dropped by Electra Records without releasing an album.

1996   Signed by Columbia Records. Collaborates with Jermaine Dupre and Wyclef Jean on their first album entitled *Destiny's Child*.

1997   "Killing Time" a track from their first album, is chosen for the *Men in Black* soundtrack.

1998   *Destiny's Child* is released, and one million copies are sold. Soft and Beautiful Botanicals Hair product contract. Concert tours with Wyclef Jean and Boyz II Men.

1999   Second album, *The Writing's On the Wall*, goes multi-platinum. "Independent Women Part I" chosen for the *Charlie's Angel* soundtrack. LeToya and LaTavia send letter disaffirming Mathew Knowles as their manager.

2000   Farrah Franklin and Michelle Williams replace LeToya and LaTavia. Ex-members file lawsuit against band and Mathew Knowles. Five months later Farrah Franklin leaves the group and Destiny's Child remains a trio.

2001   Third album, *Survivor,* is released. Christmas album *8 Days of Christmas* released. The group appears on *Saturday Night Live*. Headlines in the MTV *Total Request Live* Tour. Beyoncé appears in MTV's *Hip Hopera: Carmen*. Kelly records solo song for Chris Rock movie, *Down to Earth*.

ACCOMPLISHMENTS

Discography

1998   *Destiny's Child*

1999   *The Writing's On the Wall*

2001   *Survivor*
        8 Days of Christmas

Awards

1999   Three Lady Soul Train Awards for the album, *Destiny's Child*.
        Best Single, Best Album, Best New Artist.

2000   Sammy Davis Jr. Award for Entertainer of the Year
        Four Billboard Awards
        NAACP Image Award
        International Dance Music Award for "Independent Women."
        Blockbuster Entertainment Award—Favorite Group of the
            Year and Favorite R&B Group
        Soul Train Lady of Soul Awards—Best R&B Soul Single,
            "Say My Name"
        Best R& B Soul Album of the Year, *The Writing's on the Wall*.
        American Music Award—Favorite R&B Band.

2001   MTV Music Video Award—R & B Video
        BET Award—Best Female Group
        NAACP Image Award
        Four Grammy nominations for *Survivor*
        Two Grammy Awards for "Say My Name" from the album,
            The Writing's on the Wall
        Four MTV Music Video nominations

FURTHER READING

Dunn, Jancee. "A Date With Destiny." *Rolling Stone*, May 24, 2001.

Kenyatta, Kelly. *Yes, Yes, Yes: The Unauthorized Biography of Destiny's Child*. Hollywood: Busta Books, 2000.

MacDonald, Evelyn. "Destiny's Child and Their Voice as Survivors." *Miami Herald*, April 3, 2001.

Neuman, Marie. "Survivors." *Honey*, May 2001.

Norment, Lynn. "The Untold Story of How Tina and Mathew Knowles Created the Destiny's Child Gold Mine." *Ebony*, September 2001.

Websites

www.destinyschild.com

www.absolutely.net/destiny/

www.mtv.com

ABOUT THE AUTHOR

DAWN FITZGERALD is a freelance writer from Cleveland, Ohio. In addition to this book, she has written the biographies of Angela Bassett and Ben Stiller for Chelsea House. Dawn earned a BA from the University of Rochester and an MA from John Carroll University. She lives in Ohio with her husband, John, and her children, Ryan and Brynn.

INDEX